First Facts

The LIFE and TIMES of
Abraham Lincoln
and the U.S. Civil War

by Marissa Kirkman

CAPSTONE PRESS
a capstone imprint

First Facts are published by Capstone Press,
1710 Roe Crest Drive, North Mankato, Minnesota 56003
www.mycapstone.com

Library of Congress Cataloging-in-Publication Data
Names: Kirkman, Marissa, author.
Title: The life and times of Abraham Lincoln and the US Civil War / by
    Marissa Kirkman.
Description: North Mankato, Minnesota : Fact Finders Books, an imprint of
    Capstone Press, 2017. | Series: First facts. Life and times | Includes
    bibliographical references and index.
Identifiers: LCCN 2016014661 | ISBN 9781515724742 (library binding) |
    ISBN 9781515724827 (pbk.) | ISBN 9781515724865 (ebook pdf)
Subjects: LCSH: Lincoln, Abraham, 1809–1865—Juvenile literature. |
    Presidents—United States—Biography—Juvenile literature. | United
    States—History—Civil War, 1861–1865—Juvenile literature.
Classification: LCC E457.905 .K495 2017 | DDC 973.7092 [B] –dc23
LC record available at https://lccn.loc.gov/2016014661

Editorial Credits
Charmaine Whitman, designer; Tracy Cummins, media researcher;
Tori Abraham, production specialist

Image Credits
Capstone Press: 5; Getty Images: Thomas Allom, 9; Library of Congress:
Cover Right, 1, 4, 8, 12, 14, 15, 17 Left, 17 Right; North Wind Picture
Archives: 7, 11, 21; Shutterstock: Apostrophe, Design Element, Everett
Historical, Cover Left, 13, 19

Printed in the United States of America in North Mankato, Minnesota.
009683F16

Table of Contents

A New Country 4

Making New Laws 6

Frontiers and Factories 8

Plantations in the South 10

A Dividing Country 12

A New Leader 14

The Civil War Begins 16

Freeing the Slaves 18

The End of the War 20

After the War 21

Glossary 22

Read More 23

Internet Sites 23

Critical Thinking Using the Common Core 24

Index 24

A New Country

In the 1800s, the United States was a young country. Less than 100 years before, the U.S. fought a war with Great Britain and won its **freedom**. Since then, the country grew by adding **territories** and states. Many people lived and worked on the **frontier**. Abraham Lincoln was one of them. He was born on February 12, 1809. He grew up in a log cabin on the Kentucky frontier.

freedom—the right to live the way you want

territory—an area connected with or owned by a country that is outside the country's main borders

frontier—the far edge of a country, where few people live

Lincoln's log cabin

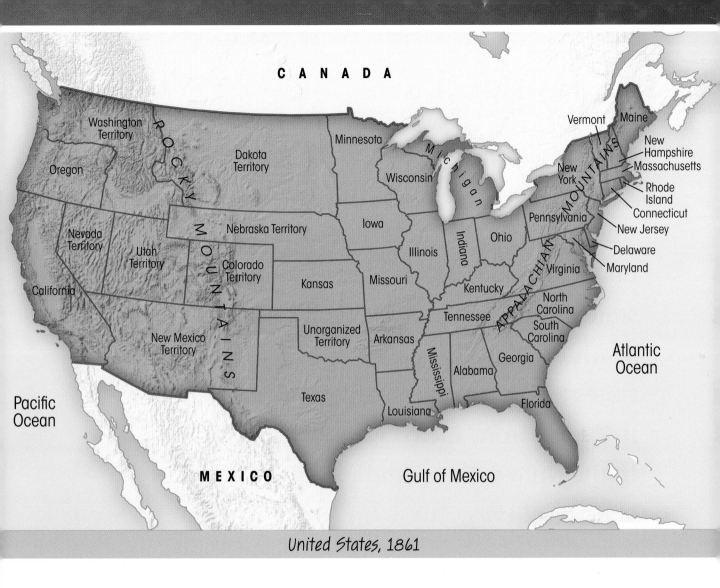

United States, 1861

Fact: In 1800 there were 16 states in the United States of America. By 1861 the country had grown to have more than 30 states.

Making New Laws

Early leaders wrote laws for states to follow in the U.S. Constitution. The leaders could not decide on laws about **slavery**. They decided to let each state make its own laws. States in the south made laws to allow slavery. Most states in the north made laws against it. People from Africa were brought to the United States and forced to work as **slaves**.

---

slavery—the owning of other people; slaves are forced to work without pay

slave—a person who is owned by another person

Frontiers and Factories

During the 1800s, many people moved west to new U.S. territories. They set up farms and built towns. A lot of cities in the north had factories. Many people worked in factories to make things the new country needed.

Lincoln worked in many jobs as a young man to help his family. As an adult, he was **elected** to the Illinois state **government**.

Lincoln was elected in 1846.

---

elect—to choose someone as a leader by voting

government—the group of people who make laws, rules, and decisions for a country or state

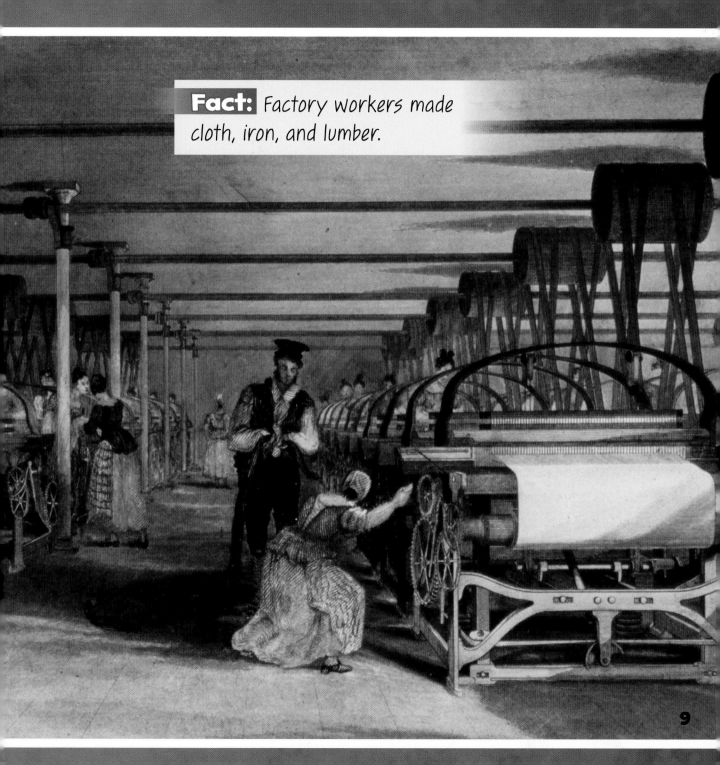

Fact: Factory workers made cloth, iron, and lumber.

Plantations in the South

In the south, people grew **crops** on large farms, called plantations. Cotton was the most common crop because it was needed to make cloth. Plantation farmers needed slaves to work in the fields. Slaves worked in the fields all day picking cotton and other crops. They were not paid for the hard work that they did. They were not allowed to leave the plantation.

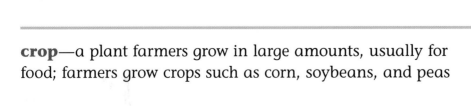

crop—a plant farmers grow in large amounts, usually for food; farmers grow crops such as corn, soybeans, and peas

Fact: Men and women held as slaves depended on the plantation owners for food, clothing, and places to live.

A Dividing Country

Most plantation owners did not take very good care of their slaves. Many slaves escaped by running away to the north. Lincoln was one of many people in the north who did not think slavery was right. He and others wanted to pass laws against slavery across the country. But people in the south wanted to keep their way of life. They felt states had the right to choose to keep slavery.

Fact: Harriet Tubman was a slave who escaped to freedom in the north. She went back to the south many times to help bring other slaves to freedom in the north.

Harriet Tubman

Many slaves waited until nighttime to escape in the dark.

A New Leader

Lincoln was elected as president in 1860. When Lincoln took office in 1861, he did not want the country to break apart.

States in the south did not want Lincoln to make slavery against the law. They left the United States to make their own country. They named it the **Confederate States of America.** They chose Jefferson Davis as their president.

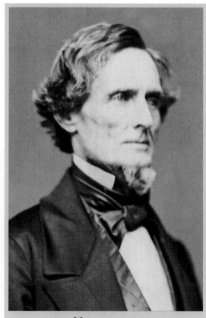

Jefferson Davis

Fact: At first, seven states left to create the Confederate States of America. They were Alabama, Florida, Georgia, Louisiana, Mississippi, South Carolina, and Texas. Later, Arkansas, North Carolina, Tennessee, and Virginia also joined.

Abraham Lincoln

Confederate States of America—the group of southern states that fought against
the northern states in the Civil War

15

The Civil War Begins

The Civil War began in 1861 when the Confederate Army attacked **Fort** Sumter in South Carolina. Americans were now at war with each other. In the south, the Confederate Army had many strong soldiers. In the north, the **Union** Army was able to get **supplies** and weapons from the many factories. Many railroad tracks were in the north, which also helped the Union Army.

Fact: Confederate soldiers wore gray uniforms. Union soldiers wore dark blue uniforms.

Union
soldier

Confederate
soldier

fort—a place built to be strong to keep the people living there safe from attack

Union—the northern states that fought against the southern states in the Civil War

supplies—materials needed to do something

Freeing the Slaves

Lincoln had not wanted a war, but he was against slavery. He wrote the Emancipation Proclamation. This law would free all slaves in the south if the Union won the war. Many free black Americans in the north fought for the Union. Some slaves escaped from the south and joined the Union Army. About 180,000 black Americans fought as Union soldiers. They were fighting for their freedom.

Fact: The Emancipation Proclamation became a law on January 1, 1863.

Many black Americans joined the Union Army.

The End of the War

Thousands of Americans on both sides died in battle during the war. One large battle took place in Gettysburg, Pennsylvania, in 1863. After three days of fighting, the Union Army won this battle. This battle was a turning point for the Union. Two years later, the Confederate Army **surrendered**. The war was over, and the United States was one country again.

Fact: Lincoln gave the Gettysburg Address on November 19, 1863, in the place where the battle was fought. This important speech honored the soldiers who had died in the war.

surrender—to give up or stop fighting a battle

speech—a talk given to an audience

After the War

The Civil War was an important event in the history of the United States. About 600,000 American soldiers died in the war on both sides. As president, Lincoln was able to end slavery. After the war was over, a law was passed that banned slavery across the nation. But Lincoln never saw the end of slavery. He was shot on April 14, 1865, and died the next day. Lincoln is remembered as the leader who kept the country together.

Glossary

Confederate States of America (kuhn-FE-der-uht STATES UHV uh-MER-i-kuh)—the group of southern states that fought against the northern states in the Civil War

crop (KROP)—a plant farmers grow in large amounts, usually for food; farmers grow crops such as corn, soybeans, and peas

elect (i-LEKT)—to choose someone as a leader by voting

fort (FORT)—a place built to be strong to keep the people living there safe from attack

freedom (FREE-duhm)—the right to live the way you want

frontier (fruhn-TEER)—the far edge of a country, where few people live

government (GUHV-urn-muhnt)—the group of people who make laws, rules, and decisions for a country or state

slave (SLAYV)—a person who is owned by another person

slavery (SLAY-vur-ee)—the owning of other people; slaves are forced to work without pay

speech (SPEECH)—a talk given to an audience

supplies (suh-PLIZE)—materials needed to do something

surrender (suh-REN-dur)—to give up or stop fighting a battle

territory (TER-i-tor-ee)—an area connected with or owned by a country that is outside the country's main borders

Union (YOON-yuhn)—the northern states that fought against the southern states in the Civil War

Read More

Blashfield, Jean F. *Slavery in America.* A True Book. New York: Children's Press, 2012.

Gilpin, Caroline Crosson. *Abraham Lincoln.* Readers Bios. Washington, D.C.: National Geographic, 2012.

Stanchak, John E. *Civil War.* Eyewitness Books. New York: DK Publishing, 2015.

Internet Sites

FactHound offers a safe, fun way to find Internet sites related to this book. All of the sites on FactHound have been researched by our staff.

Here's all you do:

Visit *www.facthound.com*

Type in this code: 9781515724742

 **Super-cool stuff!** Check out projects, games and lots more at **www.capstonekids.com**

Critical Thinking Using the Common Core

1. Why did states in the south leave to make their own country when Lincoln was elected president? (Key Ideas and Details)

2. The Union was able to get supplies from factories in the north. How did the railroad help the Union Army? (Integration of Knowledge and Ideas)

Index

Civil War, 16, 18, 20, 21
  start of, 16
  end of, 20
Confederate Army, 14, 16, 17, 20
Davis, Jefferson, 14
factories, 8, 9, 16
laws, 6, 12, 14, 18, 21
  on slavery, 6, 12, 18, 21
  Emancipation Proclamation, 18

Lincoln, Abraham, 4, 8, 12, 14, 18, 20, 21
  birth of, 4
  death of, 21
  presidency, 14, 18, 20, 21
plantation, 10, 11, 12
slavery, 6, 12, 14, 18, 21
slaves, 6, 7, 10, 11, 12, 13, 18
Tubman, Harriet, 12
Union Army, 16, 17, 18, 20